Printed in the Un
All rights reserve

This book is protected under the International Copyright Laws and the copyright laws of the United States of America. Contents and/or cover may not be reproduced in whole, or in part, in any form without the express written consent of the Author and Publisher.

Copyright © 2018 by April L. Ervin, MBA

Credits:
Book cover:
Nicole Powell, NPinspired Design, LLC
www.npinspired.com

Editor:
Angela M. Smith, Nataph Consulting
NataphConsulting@outlook.com

The Burnout Factor™
ISBN-13: 978-1720667520
(P) & © 2018
April L. Ervin
www.aprilervin.com

TABLE OF CONTENTS

Acknowledgements

Introduction

Chapter 1: Make Ending *"Burnout"* a Strategic Priority

Chapter 2: Stop Expecting You (Or Anyone Else) To Have Superhuman Powers

Chapter 3: Make Taking Care of **YOU** Your First Priority

Chapter 4: Realize the Transformative Power of *"Doing Less"*

Chapter 5: Redefine Your Definition of Success

Chapter 6: Conduct an Organizational Health Assessment

Chapter 7: Develop a Support Network (You Are Not in This Alone)

Conclusion

Recommended Reading

About the Author

ACKNOWLEDGEMENTS

This book is dedicated to every leader who has struggled to find balance in their professional and personal lives.

While I share my book from the perspective of an education and nonprofit leader, the guidance and tools are of great benefit for **_all_** leaders.

I am humbled by the journey God has brought me through. I am grateful to be a testament and share my learnings for the good of others.

Be Blessed.

INTRODUCTION

The commitment to be of service in the field of education is not just a profession...it is a calling. As education and nonprofit leaders, we are called to minister to the souls of the *"least and the left out"*. We are called to be servant leaders and examples for many to follow. More than 15 years ago, I felt that calling when I transitioned from my career in corporate America to the public sector. I was highly idealistic and hopeful of the impact I might have on the lives of children. Having managed countless difficulties in my own family - seeing my young nephew struggle in the traditional public-school system - I stepped into my calling committed to making a difference. I was extremely fortunate in my own public-school experience and wanted the same for others. (I often say I attended the best elementary school there is – thank you School #86). I firmly believed every child should have that same opportunity.

As I worked to bring my newfound calling and passion to fruition, I was hit with some harsh realities. I began to understand the depth of educational disparities we faced and was exposed to the plethora of problems. While not insurmountable, these issues represented a greater feat than I initially realized. Despite the barriers, I forged ahead and fully embraced my calling.

As I moved forward, I spent many years in a place of self-sacrifice – all for the sake of transforming lives. Days bled into evenings; evenings into weekends and weeks felt like months. I was consumed by my commitment to *"the call"*. Ultimately, my dedication came at a significant price and began to feel more like a burden. It drained the life out of my very being and left me spiritually, mentally, physically, and emotionally depleted. Depleted by attempting to meet the needs of many while neglecting my own. I became exhausted by the imbalance, dysfunction, and pervasive toxicity across education and the nonprofit community that supported it.

As a result, my health was severely affected. I was left with no other choice but to step away from my calling. However, my suffering resulted in an unexpected blessing that necessitated a major shift in my life. I was blessed with a total life transformation. One that brought greater clarity of my true calling; a transformation that resulted in my living a personal and professional life of peace, balance, and optimal health; a transformation which helped me realize it was still possible to heed my original call. However, to do so required a radically different approach.

After an extended hiatus, I returned to my original calling in education and nonprofit leadership with a renewed perspective. I returned fully healed and strengthened: mind, body, spirit and soul. I returned with a desire and commitment to support others who had heeded the same call now exhausted by the toxicity of the environments in which they served. I was adamant that as a community, we needed a substantial paradigm shift in how we worked to achieve our missions. My prayer was if we openly acknowledged our struggles, we could begin to change. We could begin to heal. Unwavering in my belief, I firmly believed until we made a concerted and deliberate effort to more holistically support our education and nonprofit leaders we would continue to struggle to achieve sustainable change on behalf of children and communities. Until we made a dedicated effort to the social and emotional development of adults, we would continue to face the same challenges.

Over the years, I've seen leaders work themselves sick all in the name of children and mission. I've seen them sacrifice themselves, their families, and their futures to meet arbitrarily designed metrics and goals. I've witnessed the damaging impact of political agendas that caused well-meaning individuals to take actions they would have never fathomed. I've seen irrational commitments to rapid growth and expansion result in thankless sacrifice. I've even seen high levels of dysfunction and egos outweigh what was best for the children we served. I've watched how personal matters crept into the professional, negatively impacting the leader and organization they led.

This mindset breeds a level of dysfunction that is indelible. As result, well-meaning and committed leaders become enveloped in the toxicity – ultimately resulting in the mental, spiritual and physical depletion of those charged with the monumental task of leading change. This depletion has severely impacted the likelihood of sustainable success for the children we are called to serve.

Consequently, a recurring cycle of high turnover, burnout, and the weakening of quality leadership has unfortunately been birthed. A mentality of *"churn and burn"* has become common at every level in far too many schools and nonprofit organizations.

Far too many highly qualified and valued leaders make the difficult decision to leave the education and nonprofit community after years of self-sacrifice. Many leave having been beat down by a system that is set up for failure; they've lost that fire from their initial calling, and long to salvage any semblance of a life. These leaders leave out of weariness and a lack of hope. More disheartening some - like me - abandon their calling due to deteriorating health. Even more damaging are those who remain and are overwhelmed with constant stress and frustration they face daily. Again, in no way do I exclude myself from these leaders. As a former Executive Director of a rapidly growing nonprofit organization, I had my own struggles and made my share of mistakes. However, my heart never changed. Just like every other leader, I truly believed I could still make a difference and was willing to do anything I could to make that a reality.

In transitioning into my consulting and executive coaching practice, a dominant amount of my time has been spent helping leaders cope with the various demands of their roles. Answering to multiple constituents – CEOs, superintendents, board of directors, managers, district leaders, staff, parents, and the ultimate constituent – our children. Helping them meet the needs and demands of these constituents was vitally important. However, their remaining well-balanced was even more critical.

Albert Einstein once said: **"*insanity is doing something over and over again and expecting a different result*"**. With no disrespect, many of us are living in a state of insanity. Day in and day out, we do what we know in our hearts and souls is not best for us. Yet, subconsciously we hope and believe that things will miraculously change. Unfortunately, sanity and balance are lost in the drive for achievement and progression. Again, I do not exclude myself as I too have struggled with bouts of insanity on multiple occasions.

Through my work, I came to realize many of the matters we face are not children issues; they are adult issues. Therefore, I adamantly believe until we as leaders are effectively supported and fully restored, we will continue to struggle to achieve the success we desire. Without a focus on holistic restoration, a culture of constant burnout will remain the accepted norm. We must begin to focus on healing at our core to end this cycle of dysfunction. We must establish a new foundation of taking the best care of our whole self **_FIRST_**, to sustain the impetus of our original calling.

It is this strong belief that has called me back into the education and nonprofit sector. Having achieved a sustained level of health, peace, and balance, I have returned with a sincere passion to help other leaders do the same. Moving from a place of self-sacrifice to a place of professional and personal sustainability. I resolutely believe I have a responsibility to share the lessons I've learned and support others diligently working to be of service. I am fully committed to helping education and nonprofit leaders – **_sustain their leadership and their life_**. With that spirit of service, I offer this book as gift to all who read it. My sincere hope and prayer is you will continue to fulfill your mission and purpose from a place of peace and once and for all – eliminate **The Burnout Factor** ™ in your life.

Sincerely,
April L. Ervin, MBA
Chief Peace Officer
Sustainable Leadership, LLC

CHAPTER 1

Make Ending *"Burnout"* a Strategic Priority

Strategic: Carefully designed or planned to serve a purpose or advantage.

Priority: A thing that is regarded as more important than another.

Far too many education and nonprofit leaders struggle with burnout. It is as if through serving others burnout is a rite of passage and sometimes worn as a badge of honor. When we seek to serve *"the least, the lonely, and the left out,"* a life of imbalance and constant sacrifice seems to come with the job. It appears to be the expectation that we sacrifice our lives in our desire to impact every child and family we touch. We sincerely pride ourselves for our commitment to making a difference. The challenge is in this commitment someone extremely important gets lost – **we do**.

Between the long hours, extensive travel, politics and organizational dysfunction, we often wonder if our original reason for choosing this path is worth it. In my time in leadership, I worked to convince myself that it would be worth it in the end. That if I could just push through a few more weeks and months, I would eventually have time to take better care of myself. I worked most Sundays hoping that my Mondays would somehow be less hectic. Hopeful I might have a better handle on the coming week. Well, I'm sure you know the outcome. No matter how much I worked on the weekend, my Mondays were no better. A new week always brought a new set of challenges. The only real result was the loss of my weekend.

I ended most Sundays having completely forgotten the sermon preached at church. I greeted Monday morning tired and grouchy rather than well rested and at peace. I often remained in a constant state of déjà vu with Sundays feeling like Wednesdays and Saturdays non-existent. It took a dramatic shift for me to break that cycle. My hope and prayer is I can support you in doing the same.

So, exactly how do we make ending burnout a strategic priority? The same way we approach any other goal. With a clearly defined strategy. I purposely termed this a "strategic priority" because it will take real planning to achieve this goal. Just as we develop strategic plans to increase academic achievement or reach fundraising goals – we must do the same for ourselves. We must maintain a steadfast dedication to achieve this desired outcome. Embracing this *"laser-like"* focus will soon make burnout a thing of the past.

A critical first step is getting to the root cause of our burnout. In some cases, the root cause might be our current position/role. Others might be a toxic and dysfunctional work culture. It might also be the unrealistic expectations our managers or even we place on ourselves. Oftentimes, it's a combination of these things and more. Whatever the root cause, I promise you it is possible to develop a clear plan to cease burnout in your life. We must use the same effective planning strategies we use in our work for our own personal welfare.

Recommendation #1:
Develop a Clear Plan

Habakkuk 2:2 ~ Write the vision and make it plain.

What is not purposely documented is rarely achieved. Whether it's goals, metrics, benchmarks, or academic achievement targets – clear planning and documentation is pivotal to achieving our goals. Once these are set, advocate with your manager to integrate these new goals into your overall performance goals. Organizational buy-in is important. However, whether your boss or organization buys-in or not, **these must become non-negotiables for YOU.** You are not seeking their permission, you are advocating for your own sustainability as a leader. I know this might all sound a little out there, but somebody must step up to begin to shift our work cultures – why not you?

Sustaining your leadership and your life must, above all, be YOUR strategic priority. Think of the gifts and talents you bring to your organization. How hard you work and go above and beyond in all you do. With that in mind, you can move forward with the confidence knowing what an asset you truly are. Remember *"we have not because we ask not"*. If you don't ask for the support and buy-in, you'll never receive it.

Keep it Simple

Because I am a "checker-offer" (I'm sure that's not a word, but you get my point), I must write down my goals, and check them off as they are achieved. I am a visual learner, so I also must place them where I can see them as a constant reminder. For me seeing is believing. You can use the chart on the next page as an example. I'm sure there are several apps to track goals (as my millennial team members often remind me – there is an app for everything). Choose what works best for you. I'm a bit "old school" and still tend to use pen and paper. To hold yourself accountable, I also recommend scheduling them on your calendar. Doing so will serve as a constant reminder of your commitment to self.

| MAKE ENDING BURNOUT A STRATEGIC PRIORITY ||||
| **Affirmation:** *"I will end "burnout" in my life. I refuse to live overworked, exhausted and stressed out another day!"* ||||
Goal(s)	Start Date	Status (√)	Progress/ Reflections
1. Schedule daily *"peace breaks"* at work; two (2) 20-minute breaks throughout the day; close your door or find a quiet space – put up a *"do not disturb"* sign.			
2. Commit to leaving the office/school early at least once a week.			
3. Turn off your work phone/email after 7 p.m. each night.			
4. Turn off your personal phone/email/social media after 8 p.m. each night (spend time with your family)			
5. Schedule weekly lunch/outing with your spouse/friends			
6. Schedule time for daily exercise (1/2 hour or more)			
7. Schedule weekly self-care time – what feeds your spirit (e.g., massage, meditation, movies).			

Again, this is only an example. Make this your own. Detail goals and priorities that work best for your daily life. Doing so is key.

Proverbs 18:21 ~ The tongue has the power of life and death, and those who love it will eat its fruit.

Speak Life

In addition to this tool, I have also found daily affirmations to be powerful tools reaffirming my goals for a balanced healthier life. Affirmations are designed to reaffirm our focus and commitment. From experience, I've learned what we speak will happen – the positive and the negative. Our words have power. So, I encourage you to speak positivity over your life and work. Words that build you up and not tear you down; words that inspire creativity and not frustration and stagnation.

I recommend declaring your affirmations every day as a reminder of your commitment to your goals. Again, while some of this might seem "out of the box,"

I assure you it works. Yes, even in our professional lives. ***It is beyond time to make "burnout" a distant memory in your life.*** Remember, those that fail to plan, plan to fail. Stay committed to your plan.

<u>Recommendation #2:</u>
Take a No Excuses Approach

For all of this to work we must take a *"no excuses approach"*. We cannot allow anyone to stand in the way of making this a reality. I'm sure we can all relate to the commitment it takes to lose weight, right? Well, this is no different. We must build our stamina and strengthen our *"ending burnout muscles"*. ***If YOU don't put YOU first – believe me no one else will.*** We must eliminate those excuses rather than letting them derail us. It's very easy to become comfortable with our excuses. *"I just have too much on my plate to take "peace breaks" during the day; or I can't leave the office/school early there is too much to* do; or I can't turn my phone off at night that's when I catch up on my emails".

Again, I empathize with you. I made those same excuses. And guess what, that did nothing but open the door to my own severe *burnout*. Continuing to accept those excuses will only keep us in the same place of struggle. I promise you, taking a *"no excuses approach"* – by any means necessary – will be worth it in the end.

Recommendation#3:
Set Clear Boundaries
(Professionally and Personally)

A huge issue that contributes to burnout is the lack of clear **boundaries**. A **boundary** is defined as a line that marks the limits of an area; a dividing line. The key words here are "a dividing line". We must establish a dividing line between our professional and personal lives. Setting boundaries and making them clear to others is vitally important to ending burnout. If we allow others to disregard our boundaries, our path towards burnout is practically guaranteed. Do not lose heart. It is always possible to re-route our paths and move towards balance.

Now, let's talk about something innate to our personalities – we are givers. Givers are people who often over-commit to doing for and giving to others from a place of excess. As education and nonprofit leaders, we have such a commitment to achieving our mission we are willing to put ourselves on the backburner. With that giving spirit, our boundaries often become blurred.

Take a moment to reflect on a few questions: (1) How often do you take phone calls or check your email in the evening or on the weekends? (2) How many times are you interrupted at work to address issues that you are not really your responsibility? (3) How often are you constantly expected to drop everything to respond to ***urgent*** problems? (4) How many times do you have to cancel social plans because you are still working?

_____

_____

_____

_____

_____

_____

_____

_____

These are clear examples of a lack of boundaries and they must cease. A boundaryless life will only lead to further fatigue and imbalance.

Setting Boundaries Takes Effort

I always remind my clients that initially setting boundaries will be difficult. There will be some resistance. As others who are accustomed to us functioning a certain way, bump up against those new boundaries – it will be uncomfortable at first. Despite the resistance you must remain steadfast. A book that helped me a great deal in this area is *"Boundaries: When to Say Yes, How to Say No to Take Control of*

Your Life", *by Cloud and Townsend*. It provides practical ways to take the necessary steps to set well-defined boundaries. Check it out; it will most certainly bless you.

Organizational Impact of Burnout

I want to also share a few thoughts on the organizational impact of burnout. Making the commitment to end burnout on an individual level is critical. However, we are also clearly impacted by the organizations we lead and work within. Changing the culture of your organization might not fully be within your control. I supportively remind you the one thing you can control, and change, is YOU. While we might not have full organizational authority, we can influence our organizations by **setting a new personal standard**. As leaders, we serve as the greatest and most visible examples in our organizations. Those around us tend to follow our lead. What we do – the good and the not so good – will be imitated. If we can prompt a shift at the leadership level, it will create a domino effect. By making a commitment at an individual level, a ripple effect will occur, encouraging others to do the same. Doing so enables us to take our leadership to the next level in the most sustainable way.

To help our organizations *"see the light,"* we must be able to demonstrate the measurable effectiveness of this new way. In my work, I help organizations see the bottom-line impact of their leaders setting clear, balanced boundaries. There is definitive evidence that a harmonious, healthier, and happier leader has a clear impact on organizational productivity. Many in the private sector (e.g., Costco, Google) have tapped into this concept. In a recent article on the happiest companies to work for, the evidence is clear (*The Happiest Companies To Work For In 2018, www.forbes.com*). Now, can you imagine the day when we see a list of the happiest nonprofits and school districts to work for? I can! And, I am dedicated to making that a reality. I invite you to join me on this journey.

CHAPTER 2

Stop Expecting You (Or Anyone Else) To Have Superhuman Powers

2 Corinthians 12:9 ~ My grace is sufficient for you, for My power is made perfect in weakness.

I learned the very hard way - *Superwo(man) is a myth, she (or he) does not exist.* We may think we have superhuman powers, and sometimes it feels as if we do (that's often just exhausted adrenaline). Allow me to slightly divert for just a moment. So, I am a superhero movie fan (strangely enough – don't judge me). I loved the power and uplift many felt from the recent Black Panther, Avengers and Wonder Woman movies. Can you imagine the possibilities if we really did have their gifts and strength? We'd be unstoppable! Or, what if we could turn it on-and-off like the Hulk? Ready to battle and destroy anything standing in our way. Those might seem like elementary examples, but the truth is we and others expect us to have the physical and mental stamina of these fictional superheroes.

The unrealistic expectations of superficial powers will sustain us for a period. But, I promise you incessantly running on fumes will catch up with us. We must make a concerted effort to respect our own limits and realize those limitations do not make us weak. They, on the contrary, display our authentic strength. Limitations help us realize we were never meant to, nor can we, do it all on our own. When we try to accomplish things alone, we do ourselves and others a disservice. We also do a disservice to the only one who truly has *"superhuman"* powers – God.

The above scripture (2 Corinthians 12:9) has been my consistent help when I have felt depleted. A Divine reminder that what we might perceive as weakness is really a time for God to step in and do what we can't. This reminder frees us from struggling to save the world, our organizations, those we lead and the students and families we serve.

Recommendation #1:
Be Realistic in Your Expectations of Yourself and Others

I'm sure "realistic expectations" sound like a foreign concept to most. For many years, they were for me too. However, this is essential to sustaining our leadership and our lives. Unrealistic expectations set us up for constant struggle and ultimate failure. I'm sure you're probably thinking, "It's not me! It's my boss; it's my organization!" You are partially right. Yes, those we work for need a reality check, of what their leaders and teams can reasonably accomplish without completely exhausting themselves. Although setting *"stretch goals"* and moving from *"good to great"* are vitally important to many of our missions – constantly being stretched beyond our limits is not. As leaders, we must be cognizant of this and remember that we cannot do it all. Most importantly, we must be willing to "manage up" and let those we report realize the same.

With great empathy, I recognize that the expectations you deal with are not completely self-imposed. Many of these expectations are the push of other people. However, I emphasize you must be willing to speak up and push back when others place unrealistic expectations on you, your teams, and the goals that you are responsible for achieving. You must take courage and stand your ground. I know this will not be easy. But, standing firm on your own behalf will serve as a powerful example to those you lead.

Pushed Beyond Our Limits

We must remember, we are only one person. We just cannot do it all. I personally placed very unrealistic expectations on myself in many aspects of my leadership and my life. Thus, my own journey of extreme burnout. I constantly pushed myself beyond what was humanly possible all in the name of giving back. This issue was not only in my leadership role but in my personal life as well. With those unrealistic expectations continually hanging over my head, I spent most of my days, weeks, months and years running on fumes. I hit what I call my *"brick wall"* moment. I came to a place where changing was no longer an option. It was a mandate. I sincerely, want to help you avoid your *"brick wall"* moment by beginning to shift your mindset and expectations of self.

No matter the circumstances, we must become comfortable with saying "No". Most of the time, it might be "not at this time" or "it's more feasible at a later date". You must develop the resolve to set your parameters on deadlines that you are required to meet. I did this often and was at times viewed as obstinate by my direct manager. However, I was determined to not be subjected to unrealistic expectations and arbitrary deadlines. I also worked to protect the sanctity of my team by setting clear boundaries and expectations so that we could enjoy what we were called to do. While successful at supporting my team in setting more realistic expectations, the one person I momentarily forgot about was me. I was constantly re-assessing my own focus. A continual process and vitally necessary.

Recommendation #2:
Re-Assess Your Organization's Perception of Leadership

Clearly determining how we, and our organizations, define leadership is important to ensure that we have communities of viable leaders. Take a moment to reflect on the following: (1) What is your organization's perception of leadership? (2) How do you personally define a strong leader? (3) Is a sign of a strong leader, someone who is willing to sacrifice all for the good of the cause? (4) Do you empower leadership in your entire team?

_____

_____

_____

_____

_____

_____

From my experience, the word leadership has different meanings. I firmly believe that each of us are blessed with innate leadership skills that we hone over time. The challenge is that regardless of our experiences in leadership, we, at times, struggle with believing in our own abilities based on outdated definitions of leadership.

Forms of Leadership

Some view leadership solely from a hierarchical approach; a top-down perspective where all decision-making flows through one person. Based on my experience, this is the most ineffective way to lead. Others interpret leadership from an overly collaborative approach, always including the input and insights of the group. While this can be a more beneficial form of leadership, it too has its challenges. Being overly collaborative can lead to what I call *"analysis paralysis"*. Overthinking a situation and dragging out decision-making. While others view leadership as much more fluid with a diversity of individuals taking on leadership roles, at different times for different purposes.

A recent client shared with me her perspective on leadership that spoke strongly to what I view as the ideal. She regarded her role as that of an orchestra conductor. As the leader of her organization, her job was to bring out the absolute best in each person she led; to leverage their innate skills and talents at the most opportune times. Each person played their individual instrument gracefully – making beautiful music together – confident in their own gifting, valued and focused on having the best performance. Now, that sounds like a beautiful visual of ideal leadership.

Surround Yourself with Leaders

One of the greatest lessons I've learned as a leader is to surround myself with people whose strengths are my weaknesses. For example, in a former role I was responsible for training and developing principals. At the time, I didn't have a lot of education or school leadership experience. What I had I was extensive experience in leading and maximizing people. To compensate for my limited school leadership experience, I surrounded myself with a group of extraordinarily talented retired superintendents and principals. Combined, they held more than 100 years of experience leading schools. My leadership and human capital experience coupled with their depth of knowledge in educational leadership resulted in an exceptional team. In my opinion, this is a model of leadership to be replicated.

In my work, I often talk about *"distributive leadership"*. This might be considered an old concept, but another form of leadership I firmly believe in. **<u>Every person we lead is a leader in his/her own right.</u>** It is our job to enhance their leadership skills; to bolster their capabilities; and to allow them to advance in new ways. I recall hosting a leadership retreat for a school where the principal purposely selected teachers whose skills he was seeking to improve. I vividly recall the sense of accomplishment one of the teachers felt, when she had the opportunity to present to the group about some complex school data for the first time. When she completed her presentation, her face beamed with a sense of success. It was a real "aha" moment for both she and her principal. The principal saw a strength in her presentation skills and the teacher developed a greater confidence in her ability to lead a team. A reminder that we are surrounded by leaders just waiting to step up.

Our teams need the opportunity to display and hone their own leadership style. Remember, while we may lead, we are not the only leader in our organizations. Merging individual leadership skills and gifts make for a palatable and unstoppable team. This is reinforced in a recent Harvard Business Review article: "*To Reduce Burnout on Your Team, Give People a Sense of Control, www.hbr.com*". The more we empower the leaders around us, the stronger our ability to achieve our goals.

Recommendation #3:
It Is Impossible for
EVERYTHING to Be Urgent

One of our greatest struggles is constantly projecting an inflated sense of urgency. **EVERYTHING is ALWAYS urgent**. While the mission of our work is vitally important, staying in a constant state of urgency keeps us from truly being effective. It's like constantly drinking from a fire hose and wondering why we are drowning. This does nothing but set us up for an endless state of stress, frustration, exhaustion, fatigue and perceived failure. In shifting from this urgency mentality, we can more effectively achieve our missions. Although we are fully committed to the significant work that we do, our work is not a life or death situation. We are not performing a heart surgery. However, if we don't make a change – and soon – we might need heart surgery ourselves.

In my former role as an Executive Director, I recall receiving a word of guidance from my assistant while working late one night. The truth she spoke, has stuck with me to this day. We were working hard on something that needed to be provided to our national office. It was about 8:00 p.m. and I was exhausted. She peaked her head into my office and said these poignant words *"April, is anyone going to die if we don't finish this tonight?"* I could do nothing but laugh as I answered her, "NO!" She was right. While whatever we were working on was important, no one was going to die if it did not finish that night. Well, maybe me - if I didn't cease the marathons of emergency and urgency. Thankfully no more. But, God.

Learning to Be

I share all of this to help you make the choice to shift from a sense of persistent urgency. We are human *"BEINGS"* not human *"DOINGS."* Learning to **Be** more and **Do** less will strengthen your leadership abilities. It is in our being that we have greater clarity. When we take the time to be still, problems often resolve themselves. Thus, my recommendation for 20-minute *"peace"* breaks throughout the day. You would be surprised at how quickly situations resolve rather than escalate when we take a few moments to just be still. When we shift from an urgent reactionary mode to a place of proactive peace and calmness, we can think and hear more clearly. We have a more lucid understanding of the best next steps to take. If it worked for Steve Jobs, it can most certainly work for us too (*[Why The World's Best Leaders Want To 'Meditate On It', www.forbes.com](#)*). Many CEOs and executives take their own version of "peace breaks" daily. The evidence is clear, meditation and being still have a definitive impact on productivity. We should join these leaders. We would be in good company.

CHAPTER 3

Make Taking Care of <u>YOU</u> Your First Priority

Romans 12:1 ~ Therefore, I urge you, brothers and sisters, in view of God's mercy, to offer your bodies as a living sacrifice, holy and pleasing to God--this is your true and proper worship.

I'm sure this goes without saying, but I'm going to reiterate again. **<u>YOU must make taking care of YOU a priority.</u>** I can imagine that this statement gets lost in all that you are responsible for, but it is critically important that you embrace it. As leaders, we are accustomed to putting the needs of others before ourselves. Sometimes, we wear self-sacrifice like a badge of honor; exhibiting self-deprecating behavior that we justify for the sake of mission and purpose. I am here to remind you that **<u>*if you do not take the best care of yourself there is absolutely no way you truly be an effective leader*</u>**.

A Massive Wake-Up Call

I recall seeing Ariana Huffington, founder and former CEO of The Huffington Post and author of the book *"Thrive: The Third Metric to Redefining Success and Creating a Life of Well-Being, Wisdom, and Wonder"* on Oprah's SuperSoul Sunday a few years ago. In her interview, she shared her own wake-up call that lead her to start putting herself first and taking the best care of herself. She shared how she often worked seven days straight and rarely slept, spending little time with her family and daughters. One day while in her office she fell from exhaustion and hit her head on the side of her desk. Several hours later, she woke up in a pool of her own blood. I know...intense, but a powerful example!

That was her massive wake-up call to change. From that day forward, she not only changed on a personal level, but also made significant changes in her company. One change that really makes me smile is that she placed "nap rooms" in the offices of The Huffington Post. Now, team members can take spontaneous – yet strategic – naps throughout the day, which is conducive in helping them work at peak performance. Isn't this wonderful!? Can you imagine nap rooms in schools for principals and teachers to take power naps to recharge? I know it might sound crazy, but *anything is possible to those who believe.* If it's good enough for UBER, why isn't it good enough for those of us who have dedicated their lives to making life better for others? (6 Companies (Including Uber) Where It's OK to Nap, www.inc.com)

Recommendation #1:
Don't Wait For a "Brick Wall" to Fall to Make a Change

My Brick Wall Moment

In my former role, my own wake-up call came when my health began to significantly deteriorate. Only my CEO and direct manager were aware of what was occurring – primarily because the doctors had yet to get to the root cause of my health issues. This health scare sent me on a 12-year journey of dealing with physical challenges deeply rooted in my unwillingness to put myself first and take the best care of me.

This along with other reasons, was the primary reason for my transition from my former role. I had spent so many years sacrificing myself and my health, until I literally had nothing left to give. I was severely depleted spiritually, mentally, emotionally and physically. Because of God's grace and mercy, I can gratefully share I am no longer in that place. I have been blessed with a complete transformation of my body and life. I am now a testament, that it is unquestionably possible to be of service and take the best care of self. That is why I am so passionate about helping other leaders do the same.

Put Your Mask on First

This is soul-based work. We give our souls to this work committed to making a difference in the lives of children, families and communities. Given that reality, we must ensure we constantly refill our own tanks. We must *"put our masks on first"* before we can help someone else put theirs on *([Put On Your Own Mask First: The Safety of Self-Care, www.onbeing.com](www.onbeing.com))*. Again, this is not just important personally, it is fundamental for our organizations to embrace this mindset as well. As I shared earlier, our own leadership and life sustainability is highly dependent on this being a strategic priority for the organizations we serve.

Recommendation #2:
Organizations Must Buy-In and Be Willing to Support Their Leaders

As I've shared, the responsibility for sustaining our leaders does not rest solely in our hands. It is imperative that our organizations, schools and districts begin to wholeheartedly embrace this idea. While many participate in "professional" leadership development, very rarely is there any consideration given to the "personal" development of leaders. There might be a perception that personal development is not the responsibility of those we work for. I would argue just the opposite. You cannot separate the two; they are intimately intertwined.

Organizations and companies outside of our sector are progressively realizing, how important it is to embrace the personal development of their leaders. Now, when I say personal development I am referring to the mental, physical, social, emotional, and spiritual health of our leaders. This kind of development will ensure leaders do not give so much to their work, that their family, personal life and health severely suffers. I was just recently with a friend who is the head of a global beauty brand. She shared how her CEO has integrated a focus on holistic personal development and support for every leader in their organization. – to be sure they don't "burnout". Again, if it's a priority for global corporate executives, I argue we deserve the same.

We Value What We Invest In

In our work, we focus on what is measured and invested in. With that being true, I highly recommend that personal development training be integrated into our organizational budgets. While our focus is not a financial bottom line, our bottom line is the long-term sustainability of our leaders, teams and organizations – ultimately successfully impacting those we serve. I would argue this is most certainly measurable and attainable. Not investing in our leaders' personal development will directly impact productivity, and often negatively. Leaders who are constantly exhausted and overwhelmed cannot be effective. In fact, if we are truly committed to achieving the mission of our organizations, this should be implemented for the entire organization.

This will be a challenge at first. Know that sustainable change takes time. Nonetheless, if we are steadfast in our commitment, and willing to be advocates for change, lasting success will become the reality.

Recommendation #3: Be Willing to Take A "Strategic Pause"

As we move forward in the direction of organizational sustainability, there will be times when we will need to take a *"strategic pause"*. This is a purposely designated time not to pursue any new initiatives; set no new goals; and to consider discontinuing things we are currently doing. In working with teams, I often use the "Start, Stop, and Continue" tool to facilitate conversations in this area. As a community, we're pretty good at the start. We can generate numerous new ideas, plans, and programs. We can effectively assess those things that are working well and should continue. Where we fall short in is determining what we should stop doing.

Achieving Goals – By Any Means Necessary

In working with an organization with a long history in serving the community, the idea of a *"strategic pause"* was raised. However, the organization's leadership was less than receptive.

Serious concerns were raised of how that would affect the mission. Achieving goals and metrics by any means necessary was the strategic priority. The idea of discontinuing any aspect of the program was not up for discussion.

As we know, this tenacious dedication to a mission is very common. However, I argue that continually focusing on mission over people will, in the end, negatively impact what is working to be achieved. That was the case in this circumstance. An unwillingness to consider taking a *"strategic pause"* resulted in high levels of turnover and very low morale. I'm sure the direct opposite of what the leader desired.

The concept of taking a *"strategic pause"* can be challenging to implement. So, just how do we accomplish this? It takes time and is a process. We must first assess the affects before moving forward. In supporting organizations through this process, we first conduct a thorough organizational review. We assess the effectiveness of the initiatives, programs and services currently in place. We examine the costs, benefits and potential implications. Once our review is completed, we decide how extensive this *"strategic pause"* will be. In some cases, it is short-term, only a few weeks. In other cases, we make the sometimes hard decision to take 3-6 months to discontinue what we are currently doing. I know, this seems like a long time. But, trust me, at times it is vitally necessary. During that 3-6 month period, we have the opportunity for deep assessment and reflection. We have the time to breathe; making sure what we do, what we offer, is yielding the desired outcomes. We have the chance for course correction. We can address issues in our organizations and build up those we lead. We have time to listen to those that work so hard every day to serve the mission. **The ultimate outcome? A stronger, more focused, rejuvenated team ready to take the mission of our work to the next level**.

With one of my nonprofit clients, a concern was raised regarding how the board and funders would perceive this *"strategic pause"* and what would happen if they didn't achieve their annual goals? Let me emphasize, in this work, we are in a marathon not a sprint. We cannot be short-sighted and think only about the current year. We must focus on the long-term and maintain a commitment to creating sustainable organizations. Again, while not always easy to execute the long-term benefit is immeasurable. It will most certainly impact the lasting sustainability of our organizations, ourselves and those we lead.

Recommendation #4:
Take Time for Reflection

In the article I referred to earlier on CEO's and meditation, the author shared how those leaders also used journaling as a part of their daily practice. I am glad to see that I am in good company as I journal daily (at least I try to). I use my time of journaling to reflect on my daily activities, to capture my prayers, and to record my expectations for the next day. As a woman of faith, I choose to use scripture as part of my journaling, as reading and writing something inspirational motivates my spirit.

It is so very important to remain in a constant state of reflection. When we are moving at 100mph, it's difficult to reflect. I would argue that this is exactly why it's even more important to make purposeful time for reflection – to slow us down so that we can breathe again. I know it might be challenging. At the end of a hectic day, reflection is the last thing we are thinking of. Most of us are ready to just fall out in our beds and call it a night. I complete relate. While it might be an initial challenge, there is something powerfully healing about purposeful reflection. What's even more powerful is reflecting on how you want your tomorrow to be.

Envision Your Future

I learned this practice from one of Oprah's SuperSoul Sunday shows (yes, I watch that show a lot). The guests shared that before going to bed, they not only reflected on their day but wrote specific things they sought for the next day. It's been some time since I've done this, but when I did – it was pretty amazing.

Much of what I wrote the night before happened. My focus was on speaking positively over the results I wanted the next day. And, those positive results came to fruition. A pastor, I greatly enjoy shared that he leaves nothing in his life to chance. **He speaks what he seeks in his life with authority and conviction.** We can most certainly do the same. On the following page, take a moment to reflect on your day today. Equally important, write down what you want your tomorrow to be like: (1) Are managing a difficult political situation at work – write the resolution you seek. (2) Are you becoming overwhelmed with the demands and unrealistic deadlines of your manager? Think about and write down what you would prefer him/her do. (3) Is the culture of your organization causing you difficulties? Reflect on the changes you would like to see. (4) Are you having difficulty with a colleague or team member? Write down how you would like this issue to be resolved.

_____

_____

_____

_____

_____

_____

_____

_____

Remember, what we focus on in our lives will occur. The more we think and reflect on what we seek to occur, the more that reality will eventually come true.

Let It All Out

One other note, while I encourage positivity in our time of reflection, there is also something therapeutic about releasing the bad. Sometimes my journaling is a rant of my frustrations from the day. I'm sure you can relate. Sometimes you just need to let it all out. While a healthy release, I ALWAYS end my time of reflection on the positive. I truly encourage you to make journaling a part of your daily routine. Again, if it's good enough for Fortunate 500 CEO's, it's most certainly good enough for us.

Organizational Reflection

While reflection at the leadership level is vitally important, it is just as important at the organizational level. One of my favorite services I offer to my clients are off-site strategic planning and leadership retreats. I've used this practice for many years with great impact. It allows your full leadership team the opportunity to step away, reflect, and plan, unconstrained by daily responsibilities. It is also an opportunity to ensure your leadership team is on one page and conveying a cohesive vision.

As a follow-up to these retreats, I suggest establishing bi-weekly reflection calls or meetings with your leadership team. During that time, rather than focusing on the daily struggles, concentrate on how far you've come. Let your "wins" strengthen you while addressing challenges. Reflect on how you envision your future leadership pathway and the future of your organization. We cannot know where we are going if we don't take the time to reflect on where we've been.

CHAPTER 4

REALIZE THE TRANSFORMATIVE POWER OF *"DOING LESS"*

Matthew 11:28 ~ Come to me, all you who are weary and burdened, and I will give you rest.

Work Smarter, Not Harder

This next recommendation has everything to do with learning to *"work smarter and not harder"*. Again, I'm sure this might sound unrealistic when you have a hundred emails to respond to or constant emergencies flooding into your office. But remember, while it might seem urgent, it is impossible for everything to be an emergency.

As education and nonprofit leaders, there is no question about our work ethic. We work hard! Oftentimes, too hard and – with all due respect – rarely smart. There is no place for blame. This is the nature of our world. However, we can be the *barrier breakers* and begin to do things differently. The ultimate outcome will be achieving our goals while living fulfilled rather than eternally exhausted.

Recommendation #1:
Set Clear Boundaries (Again)

I share this recommendation again, because it is so vitally important to *working smarter not harder*. Working smarter has a great deal to do with setting clear boundaries. I recall a recent leadership position where I made the decision **not** to install my work email on my personal phone. For almost a full year, nothing was so urgent that I had to check my email from home. I'm sure this is hard to believe, but I assure you staying constantly connected is the opposite of setting clear boundaries. Most importantly, the lack of separation between work and home guarantees traveling down the pathway of eventual burnout.

How We Start Our Day Is How It Will End

A recent article in INC Magazine emphasizes that setting a consistent daily routine can also help us achieve the goal of working smarter and not harder ([Work Smarter, Not Harder: 10 Ways to Be More Effective at Work, www.inc.com](www.inc.com)). I personally have seen the power of having a steady morning routine. **How you start your day is how you will end your day.** If you start your day in chaos, your day will most certainly end the same. If you start your day in calm and at peace, that will carry with you throughout the day and help you deal with whatever comes your way.

I recall working with a school principal who struggled a great deal with this idea. She felt such a sense of responsibility both at home and at work, that she did not see how she could find time for herself in the morning. She was a single mom with two daughters and dealing with a very demanding superintendent. She often felt she barely had time to take a shower and get dressed, let alone time to *"be still"* in the morning before going to work. I lovingly encouraged her she needed to shift her **attitude and perspective**. If she believed she could not set a routine that would help her go into her day peacefully, then she wouldn't. The only result would be the continuous daily anxiety she had been experiencing.

Each week we added time to her morning routine to focus just on herself. As she did so, something interesting happen. After sharing with her daughters that she just needed an extra ½ hour each morning for quiet time, her daughters began to help more. Her oldest daughter began making breakfast for her little sister. That small action helped her to release the guilt of "being everything to everyone". This created space for her to reflect on how she wanted her day to go. She also shut off her cell phone, so she would not be interrupted. Slowly but surely, this became a morning routine coupled with some exercise allowed her to begin her day with greater energy and less anxiety. I share more about her journey in a 2016 LinkedIn article: Dear 'Super Mom': It's OK To Put Yourself First.

While initially a challenge, setting that simple personal boundary helped her tremendously. So much so that she began setting more boundaries professionally as well. Working smarter and setting clear boundaries does not have to be an exhaustive process (we tend to overthink things). It's the small steps that ultimately build us up and help us in our efforts to work smarter not harder – and have greater peace along the way.

Recommendation #2:
Take the Pressure Off

We Were Never Meant to Do It All

Again, while our work is important we are not performing lifesaving surgery. If it doesn't get done today, it can and will get done tomorrow. We place undue pressure on ourselves when we stress over the amount of work we can or should accomplish in a single day. I'm sure your "to-do-list" is just as mine used to be – long. I could make lists forever; but given that there are only 24 hours in a day, my lists were still never completed like I wanted them to be.

With that realization, my lists got shorter and shorter. I began to focus on the top three things I wanted to accomplish each day. Doing so made getting my work done more feasible. Sure, I had more than three things I needed to accomplish, but if I got those three things done I felt a sense of achievement and was encouraged to come back the next day and do the same. To my own surprise, the more I did this the shorter my lists became and the more I maximized my time.

As I share in the following chapter, your definition of success will dictate your progress. If you define success as getting everything done in a single day, you are setting yourself up for disappointment. ***Even if we worked 24 hours a day, 7 days a week, we still couldn't get it ALL done.*** Given that, why not give yourself a break and take a more realistic approach to your work? Remember, if we place undue pressure on ourselves our teams will mimic that same behavior.

This idea is also important when we think about establishing annual performance goals. There is no question of our commitment to achieving our missions. However, setting unrealistic goals can place undue pressure on our entire organization. I've seen it time and again where leaders set extremely aggressive goals and provide limited timeframes to achieve those goals. Doing so sets the stage for feeling as if we will never meet expectations. I'm an advocate of SMART (Specific, Measurable, Achievable, Results-Focused and Time-Bound) goal. However, I tend to change the "S" in SMART to "simple" instead of "specific". There is no need to overcomplicate our work. Some of the simplest acts can have the greatest impact.

Leave It at Work

The last thing I'll share in this section is a reminder of the impact that stress and pressure have on our personal lives. If we are constantly overwhelmed at work, it will be visible at home. That needless stress affects our relationships and the constant state of pressure makes our homes toxic as well (*The Impact of Stress on Children and Families,* www.mdmag.com). I know in our heart of hearts, this is the last thing we want for those we love. With that, we must be willing to take preventive measures to keep our homes free from work-related stress. Our goal should be stress-free organizations and stress-free homes.

Recommendation #3:
Efficiency Is Not a "Bad" Word

In my work, discussions of being more efficient is sometimes met as a foreign concept. While efficiency has not traditionally been our focus, I firmly believe it must become a priority. During my corporate days, I worked for a consulting firm that helped companies perform more efficiently and effectively. I truly enjoyed this work. I didn't realize how much it fed my spirit to look at circumstances and make them better for those charged with doing the work. This further fueled my passion for helping education and nonprofit leaders do the same.

I recognize we don't have the same resources or time of major corporations to hire management consultants. However, I would argue that we have some of the best consultants in the world – those who do this work daily. Those that teach the students, lead our programs and run our organizations. These are our *"subject matter experts"* and they know how best to increase efficiency. Sometimes it just takes being willing to listen. If we've done the work to build a competent team, we must be willing to trust in their talents, skills and abilities. As we think about ways to perform our work more effectively, we should seek out theses subject matter experts. Doing so shows our teams that we value their abilities and perspectives.

So, how do we get started with making our work more efficient and effective? Take a few moments to reflect on these questions: (1) In what ways can you be more efficient in your daily work? (2) Are their opportunities to streamline ways in which your work is done? (3) Who are your "subject matter experts" and how do you leverage them? (4) Do you actively leverage the strengths of full team?

_____

_____

_____

_____

_____

_____

_____

_____

Be Open to New Ideas

To leverage our team's expertise, we must be willing to not hold on too tightly to any part of our work. At times, as leaders we can be so attached to our work that we are unwilling to consider alternatives. While we might have done this work for many years, sometimes a fresh perspective can open our eyes to how we can do our work better.

With a focus on efficiency and effectiveness, I encourage you to obtain both internal and external feedback. Sometimes, we are so engrossed in our work, we might struggle to see opportunities for improvement. However, I guarantee you that our students, parents, funders and community members have beneficial feedback we can use. They are the receivers of our services and can best measure how effectively we are doing. Equally, we must be willing to receive the feedback even if it's not what we want to hear. Accepting this constructive feedback could make the difference in our ability to take our work to the next level.

Lastly, the best thing about efficiency and effectiveness is it supports our efforts to work smarter not harder. These efforts lessen the stress and pressure and allow us to enjoy our work even more. As we shift towards greater efficiency, our teams will reflect renewed attitudes and commitment to working together to achieve our goals; and the families we serve will have a more impactful experience. Just as stress and pressure are contagious, so are peace, balance and contentment. Making the effort to obtain the latter will generate a ripple effect; one that will leave a legacy for those who come after us. This is a goal that all leaders should seek – leaving our organizations better off than when we began.

CHAPTER 5

Redefine Your Definition of Success

Your Job Does Not Define You

As you move forward with eliminating burnout, I am going to challenge you to redefine your definition of success. While high academic achievement, reaching fundraising and strategic planning goals are important – those things do not define you. I encourage you to never define your success based on whether you achieve these goals or not. You are more than your goals, title, salary or academic achievement. Your success is based on the resilience and commitment you show every day; not on arbitrary numbers or metrics. True success should be based on your commitment to do your best and be your best amid any obstacles you face. Giving yourself the grace to know that just your sheer perseverance is an indicator of success.

It is critical to focus on the whole wo(man). What you do is only a piece of the whole of who you are.

When our work and leadership role is our sole focus...burnout is inevitable. When our work becomes all-consuming, we lose sight on what it means to truly LIVE. We were not put on this earth to just merely exist and trudge through each day. We were put on this earth to live vibrantly; *to have life and life more abundantly*. And yes, it is possible to do so and achieve this new vision of success.

When we allow our work to define us, we set ourselves up for failure that often can lead to an isolated life. When we exclude a balanced life as part of our envisioned success, we are essentially living with a distorted perspective on what it means to truly live. More than once, I've heard it said that the last thing anyone would say after we've moved on from this life is *"I wish I would have worked more"*. As shared in this Huffington Post blog post, *[10 Words You Won't Say...On Your Deathbed](#)*, when that time comes I doubt any of us would be thinking about spending more time at work.

Burnout is guaranteed when we neglect the other aspects of our lives. Without intentional focus, our personal sense of balance and fulfillment will most certainly be negatively affected. So, what is your definition of success? Take a moment to reflect: (1) Do you focus solely on your role and goal or do you take a more holistic perspective? (2) Is working more and earning more your perception of success? If it is, I challenge you to redefine your definition. I fully support my clients in career progression, just not to the detriment of their well-being.

_____

_____

_____

_____

_____

_____

_____

Setting and achieving goals are important aspects of perceived success. However, from my perspective, a true description of success is living a fulfilled, balanced life. By this I mean, a life of purpose – healthy, happy, balanced, loving, appreciating yourself and grateful for all in your life. YES! This is absolutely possible.

Mark 9:23 ~ All things are possible to those who believe.

Recommendation #1:
Create a New "Leadership Success Profile"

In my previous consulting work, I had the opportunity to work with an organization to develop what we called a **"Leadership Success Profile"**. The core of the profile was focused on professional and career characteristics. While the profile was based on building leadership capacity, I argued we needed an expanded vision to consist of a *<u>life quotient: a computation of how successful we are at living and not merely existing; achieving a level of balance and vitality on the way towards professional success.</u>*

With this idea in mind, I created a new version of this leadership success profile, focused of course on two key components: (1) _sustainable leadership_ and (2) _sustainable life_. Establishing measurable goals in each category. I encourage you to create your own version. As you go through this process, remember this is not a job description. This is your ideal vision of your new definition of success. Not just a successful professional career, but also a gratifying and balanced personal life. Below is an example of this profile.

Ending Burnout Leadership Success Profile "Sustainable Leadership"			
Measurable Goal	**Developing**	**Meets**	**Exceeds**
Purposefully Expands Leadership Capacity		X	
Sets Clear Strategic Vision for Self and Organization			X
Clearly Conveys Collaborative Vision			X
Consistently Achieves Defined Goals and Results		X	
Practices Deliberative Distributive Decision-Making	X		
Effectively Leads and Manages Talent		X	
Establishes Clear Capacity Building and Retention Strategies			X

Ending Burnout Leadership Success Profile "Sustainable Life"			
Measurable Goal	Developing	Meets	Exceeds
Establishes Clear Boundaries Between Work and Home		X	
Communicates Boundaries Internally and Externally			X
Turns Off Technology at Specific Time (e.g. Cell Phone, Email)		X	
Takes Daily "Peace Breaks"/Meditation Throughout the Day	X		
Blocks Time on Calendar for Personal Time		X	
Spends Quality Time with Family and Friends	X		
Conducts Quarterly Self-Care Retreat for Self and Team		X	

The first part of this profile is or should be standard performance objectives for every leader. These are critical focus areas as we evolve as leaders. However, what I want to support you most is creating the same type of performance objectives for your personal well-being. Again, these are only examples. They provide concrete, measurable goals to achieve greater balance and eliminate burnout.

As you develop your profile, give yourself some grace. Do not expect to immediately "exceed" in every area. Everything will not always be balanced, at first. I know! I am a recovering Type "A" too. Like anything else, this is a process. I also want to reiterate the goal of this exercise is not to add another thing to your growing list of responsibilities. The purpose is to hold yourself accountable on your journey towards eliminating burnout and achieving greater balance.

The leaders I've been blessed to support found this to be a beneficial tool. Integrating these goals into their professional and personal lives resulted in an important shift. Focusing on personal sustainability had a definitive effective. With shifts evident in every aspect of their lives – personally, professionally and organizationally. I am a personal testament to this as well. While not perfect in my own process, I have a constant eye on my professional and personal sustainability. At this stage in my life, I refuse to go backwards. I pray you get to that place as well.

Recommendation #2:
Ensure You Have the "Right" Leadership Style

Every leader has their own style of leadership. As I've shared, some firmly believe in the "top down" approach - with all decisions by the leader. Some believe in collaboration encouraging the feedback and decision-making of their teams before making decisions. While others view their leadership style as a combination of both. So, what is most common in our work? Unfortunately, the first one. Even more unfortunate is this is the most antiquated and ineffective way to lead. (*The 5 Types Of Organizational Structures: Part 1, The Hierarchy, www.forbes.com*).

Placing the Weight of the World on Our Shoulders

"Top down" leadership places undue pressure on the one individual sitting at the top of the organization. It also causes "bottlenecks" in decision-making. I know from experience the challenge of this leadership style. Early in my role as an Executive Director, I was that leader. Modeling what I saw, I felt my title dictated this style of leadership. All the while, walking around with the weight of the world on my shoulders. That was my definition of success. I had the title, I had the office and I was the **_"leader"_**. As I matured in my leadership, I came to realize my "real job" was to build the leadership capacity of those around me. I shifted from trying to control every decision to recruiting and retaining strong talent; empowering my team with the confidence to make decisions without always needing my input. I consciously worked to model this through the organization. And, while this was completely counter to my direct leader, I was grateful to create a culture of empowerment within my own team.

Everyone Is a Leader

Progressing to more of a "distributive leadership" style greatly supports our goal of long-term sustainability. Truly sustainable leaders hone the gifts of every single person they lead for the good of the organization. I recall one of my clients sharing she firmly believed everyone in her school building was a leader – from the custodian to the assistant principal. Each person played an important role in success of the school, no matter their title.

What are your thoughts on the most effective leadership style? Is it top down, bottom up, or a combination of both? Are you committed to building the leadership capacity of every individual in your organization? Or, do you feel every decision rests on your shoulders? If you answered yes to that last question, I encourage to rethink that. You can't do it all alone, and you shouldn't have to. I'm sure you have great talent surrounding you just waiting to step up. Doing so, will lift that weight off your shoulders and ultimately strengthen your organization.

In my opinion, one strong indicator of a successful leader is when a member of their team is promoted to an equivalent or higher role than their own. That is the true power of distributive leadership: empowering and building leadership capacity for the success of the individual and the organization.

Recognizing this will not be the case for everyone on our teams, but for some. That is where thoughtful succession planning comes into play.

Recommendation #3:
It's Ok to <u>NOT</u> to Take the Promotion

I know I might lose some folks with this one. And, this completely contradicts what I just shared. But hear me out. I absolutely believe in upward progression - at the right time and for the right opportunity. However, you might come to a place in your career when the sacrifices associated with "moving up the career ladder" are just too much; when the costs far outweigh the benefits. That was the case for me. At a certain point in my leadership career, the sacrifices of working long hours, weekends, and extensive travel were just too much. Doing so and trying to be *"superwoman"* in my personal life was just no longer worth it. My definition of success dramatically shifted.

As I struggled with my health, going up the career ladder was no longer my motivation. I was more motivated by trying to figure how at the age of 35, I was facing serious health issues. At a certain point, my doctor said these poignant words to me, ***"April, you have two choices: You can either find something else to do or you can manage significant issues for the rest of your life."*** My life and my future were at stake. Hearing those words, from my doctor, I immediately thought to myself, "What does she expect me to do? I've worked hard to get to this point. And more importantly, I have a mortgage, student loans, and financial responsibilities I have to take care of". With that top of mind, rather than heed her guidance, I remained in my position for another two years - rationalizing if I just hired more people I could better manage my health and responsibilities. I'm sure you can guess that was not the right solution. Despite my view of empowering others, hiring more people initially only brought more work and pressure.

Many leaders I've supported have faced the same challenge. Again, we are type "A" personalities. Society tells us that is what we're supposed to do.

Continue to move forward and upward. Work more and harder to achieve success. But, at what cost? I encourage you to use my journey as a cautionary tale. No level of promotion is worth your health and well-being. No amount of money or a new title can give you back lost time with those who mean the most in your life.

Some of the leaders I've supported made the decision to accept the promotion. While a positive career move, the personal sacrifices and at times health challenges remained. Thankfully, they had a renewed foundation before taking on the new roles. Others, like me decided the personal costs far outweighed the benefits and moved in a different direction. Still having an impact within mission-driven organizations, influencing the future of young people – just not holding that top-level position – with a greater sense of fulfillment and a much more balanced life.

While we need strong leaders guiding our schools, districts, nonprofits and communities across this country, I argue it does not have to be to their detriment. Burnout and self-sacrifice cannot continue to just be a part of doing business. Again, I encourage professional growth. But, I also want to give you permission to embrace that *it's okay to not take the promotion.* Don't let anyone make believe you are any less of a leader if you make that choice. On the contrary, doing so might open doors you could have never imagined. It certainly has for me.

CHAPTER 6:

Conduct an Organizational Health Assessment

I'm sure you've heard it said: *"we are products of our environment"*. That is so very true. We are a direct reflection of who we surround ourselves with. We often spend more time with our colleagues than our own families (let's work on reversing that). That is why it is even more important to work in a healthy culture.

As leaders, it is in our power to define our organizational environments. Again, our teams follow our lead. If we accept extreme stress, an exaggerated sense of urgency – placing purpose over people – that is the type of culture we will have. If we have issues in our organizations we know our impeding our progress, yet don't address them – it will be impossible to have a healthy organization.

Toxicity Is Unfortunately Contagious

I've both worked within and consulted with some extremely unhealthy and toxic environments. I can often sense the culture of an organization just by walking through the doors. There are always clear indicators. Sometimes it just takes briefly talking to the first person I see. A feeling of dysfunction is evident. I've developed a very low tolerance for these types of cultures. It truly saddens me to see the impact these cultures have on the people struggling to survive within them. Even more disheartening is the leader who ignores the toxicity placing the blame on those they lead.

When working with organizations, I feel a personal responsibility to improve the culture. As leaders I believe we all have that personal responsibility. This takes time, but it is possible. While not easy, the smallest actions can make a real difference. I've always struggled with the idea that this is just the way it is – that our organizations are just inherently dysfunctional. While writing, I came across an article in Psychology Today that raised this very point. In the article *"Are Nonprofit Organizations Inherently Dysfunctional?"* it appears that excessive hours, limited resources, employee dissatisfaction, low morale and high turnover comes with the territory. I find that hard to accept.

So, what do we do about this? As leaders, what roles do we play to ensure a culture of dysfunction is not the case? How do we prompt a paradigm shift from toxicity to vitality? An important first-step is to take a thorough and honest assessment of where we work.

<u>Recommendation #1:</u>
Honestly Assess Your Organization's Health

You might be saying: *"Now exactly how do I assess my organization's health?"* I have an answer for you (well actually a few). The first sign of poor organizational health can be summed up in one word – **TURNOVER**. This might seem obvious, but far too many leaders and organizations struggle to recognize high leadership and staff turnover are clear indicators of severe issues. The *"churn and burn"* mentality within the organization causes many to accept high-turnover as normal. According to the 2016 Nonprofit

Employment Practices Survey, turnover across nonprofits increased from 16% to 19% between 2013 and 2015. This might seem like a minimal increase. In personal practice, I've worked with organizations where that rate was more like 30%. In some extreme cases, 50%. At these rates, it is virtually impossible to have a healthy organizational culture. The idea of a sustainability is far from reality. Additionally, every time someone leaves the organization, critical institutional knowledge walks out the door with them.

We Must Face It to Fix It

Addressing and rectifying the underlying symptoms of ill-organizational health is imperative. When leaders choose not to do so, continual high-turnover is inevitable. Numbers of employees who leave organizations – feeling undervalued and underappreciated – with a lingering sense that the long hours, hard work, weekend commitments, and travel were all for nothing. According the article "[15 Reasons Why Nonprofit Employees Quit](#)", www.boarddirector.com, while feeling underpaid is often a reason for turnover an unhealthy culture also ranks high on the list.

Another key indicator of your organization's health is morale. With high turnover, lower morale is virtually guaranteed. Take a moment to reflect on these questions: (1) How does your team or others speak about your organization? (2) Is your team excited about executing your leadership vision, or just going through the motions? (3) If we stood next to the virtual water cooler in your office, what might we hear? Would we hear a team fully vested in achieving your organization's purpose or a team feeling as if their voice doesn't matter? (4) What do your external partners say about your organization? The answers to these questions will provide clear evidence of whether you are leading/working for a healthy or unhealthy organization. On the following page, take a moment to reflect on the organization you work within.

_____

_____

_____

_____

_____

_____

_____

One Bad Apple Spoils the Bunch

In some cases, low morale can be the result of just a few people. Toxicity within a few, can poison the whole. When we see a few team members negatively impacting morale, it is our job to immediately address those issues. What we do not address will grow. Ignoring these issues will only cause us to deal with even greater challenges in the future.

So, how do we begin to address these issues? What steps should we take to move from a toxic culture of high turnover to one of strong retention, high morale, and organizational sustainability? **The first step is to listen to our teams**. We need to be open to their feedback. While we might have a pulse of what might be going on, some things are purposely hidden. Sometimes, a simple online survey – SurveyMonkey, Poll Daddy, and Google Forms – can be a valuable tool. This simple step sincerely communicated conveys a willingness to listen and allowing others to feel heard. Once root challenges are revealed we must acknowledge those challenges and develop a clear plan to remedy them.

Another potential tool is what I call a *"burnout assessment"*. This tool enables observation and individual discussions assessing the burnout levels of our teams. This can be implemented by those in human resources as there might be a need for confidential conversations. According to an article from the Mayo Clinic, *(Job burnout: How to spot it and take action, www.mayoclinic.org)* some clear signs of burnout include: a change in attitude, lack of interest in one's work, trouble sleeping, and unexplained physical and health issues. I know these symptoms well. As a "burned out" leader, I recall not consistently sleeping for two years without the help of medication (a medication that was highly addictive and had strong side effects). Thankfully, I now sleep well every day. But, God. I strongly encourage you to keep a constant eye on potential burnout for yourself and those you lead.

I also encourage my clients conduct a *"readiness for change and happiness factor assessment."* These tools help gauge overall staff satisfaction and readiness to address what is not working. This allows us to move beyond the symptoms towards root causes. For many a *"happiness assessment"* may sound too far out of the box. Believe it or not, happiness is now being taught at many universities. Doug Smith, former CEO of Kraft Foods, experienced his own form of burnout. He now teaches a course at DePauw University: **_"Happiness: The Art of Living with Peace, Confidence and Joy."_** Through research and study, he began to understand that the most joyful people on earth have three things in common: (1) they remember the past with peace, (2) they anticipate the future with confidence, and (3) they live in the present with joy and meaning. After reading about this, I was tempted to re-enroll in undergrad just to take that course. Additionally, in 2016, Harvard opened a center focused on happiness. (*[Harvard Has a New Center for Happiness](www.theatlantic.com), www.theatlantic.com*). I firmly believe this is not just a fad, but a real and necessary focus to move from a place of burnout to peace, happiness and balance.

Recommendation #2:
Be Willing to Address Issues Head On

As I've shared before, a few negative team members can have a detrimental impact our entire organizations. As leaders, we must be willing to take a sincere and focused approach to help those individuals address their professional and personal challenges. If those issues cannot be addressed, we must be willing to make the difficult decision to counsel them out. While not an easy decision its sometimes necessary. We must consider the good of the whole over the individual.

Toxicity, at any level, must be dealt with and eradicated. Sometimes as leaders, we might be part of the problem. We must be reflective enough to address those issues as well.

What We Resist, Persists

A career of servant leadership can be fulfilling. But, as I've shared it can also be to the detriment of other parts of our lives. We are passionate about what we do; we are committed to our missions; we are committed to transforming the lives of young people and their families. It takes courage to take on these roles. Nevertheless, our focus on the mission can blind us to what is occurring right under our noses. In some cases, we might sincerely not be aware; other times, we make the choice to put our heads in the sand avoiding the issues.

According to the Center for Nonprofit Studies, "destructive leadership" is not only pervasive it is also detrimental (*"The Dark Side of Leadership"*). As leaders, we must be willing to take a reflective perspective of how we contribute to or detract from the health of our organizations. If there are challenges, we must be willing to address without blaming. And, we must hold ourselves accountable for our own actions.

Remember, our organizations are a direct reflection of our approach to leadership and our personal beliefs. Thus, we must work to be introspective leaders – continuously assessing how our leadership is impacting those we lead. We must also remember the power of our words. What we speak can either uplift or dissuade; encourage or discourage. Our teams are constantly seeking our support and approval. If we constantly focus on the challenges and what has yet to be achieved, we leave little room to celebrate progress.

<u>*Recommendation #3:*</u>
Take A Vested Interest in Those You Lead

People Matter

As we work to create sustainable organizations, we must take a vested interested in those we lead.

Unlike the private sector, we do not focus on a financial bottom-line. However, in my opinion, we have an even more important bottom-line – people. Our capital is human. Those humans are delicate gifts placed in our care. Even the strongest person on the outside has fragility within, we must remember that.

We each deal with opportunities and challenges daily. While it is not the expectation that we know the ins-and-outs of our team members personal lives, we must take a vested interest in what happens outside of the office. We must show them that we are not only concerned with their professional performance, but also their personal growth.

The most challenging leader to work for is one who is so focused on achieving goals that they lose sight of those charged with helping them reach those goals. That is not the leader we want to be. Again, I am not saying that achieving our mission, goals, and objectives are not important - they are. However, there will always be irreparable collateral damage when we do not genuinely respect the welfare of those we lead.

With a focus on investing in our people, I am going to again challenge us as leaders to be willing to take that *"strategic pause"* I discussed earlier. If we see that our teams are continually overworked and under-resourced - we must be willing to put their welfare first. This will show our teams a sincere interest in them as a whole. Taking time for reflection and assessing progress towards our strategic vision. Time that is purposely designed and dedicated to building and connecting with those we lead, as human beings (not human "doings").

<u>Recommendation #4:</u>
Develop a Clear Retention Strategy

My final recommendation in assessing the health of our organizations is to develop a clear retention strategy. High-turnover is clear evidence there is no retention strategy in place. An unfortunate impact of high-turnover is keeping us in a constant state of looking for new talent. While we often focus on recruiting and selecting talent, we rarely focus on retaining that talent. Leaving us in a vicious cycle of turnover. We must use the same strategic efforts on retaining and sustaining good talent as we do on recruiting and selecting.

So, how do we develop a retention strategy? The steps are much of what has already been shared:

1. Focus on maintaining a healthy culture
2. Proactively address challenges within the organization
3. Openly and honestly address issues within the organization
4. Take a vested interest in your team
5. Be willing to examine the root cause of high turnover
6. Provide competitive compensation and benefits
7. Build the leadership capacity of every member of your team empowering them to lead

Money Matters

Now let's talk money. A core reason for high-turnover and burnout is feeling underpaid and underappreciated. The combination of low pay and late hours takes it toll. Now, let's be candid. No one truly seeks a career in education and nonprofit for the money; financial gain is not our motive. We enter this work with a heart to serve; to leave a legacy through our work and missions. However, finances can have a detrimental impact on sustainability.

As leaders, we must be willing to advocate for fair compensation to preserve our dedicated and hard-working employees. In the private sector, it is common to conduct competitive compensation and benefits analysis to attract and retain talent. Personally, I have yet to hear school districts and nonprofit organizations consistently do the same. This is an area where we can learn from corporate America. The for-profit world is by no means perfect and most certainly has its challenges. And, in no way am I advocating that we focus on a capitalist mentality or seeing how much money we can make. While their commodity might be technology or cars, we are blessed with the most precious commodity – our youth. To cultivate this valuable resource, we should unquestionably be adequately compensated.

Employees Are in the Driver's Seat

Recently, I heard it shared that we are moving into an employee's market. Where high quality talent has multiple options. If we are committed to a true retention strategy, we must show that our organizations are one of the best options to work for. We must create environments that others want to work within, not desire to leave. Take a moment to reflect: (1) What do you as a leader or your organization do to retain high quality talent? (2) Do your teams posses a sense of appreciation or descension? (3) What could be done differently?

_____

_____

_____

I'm sure you're thinking "we just don't have the resources like for-profit companies". So, let's talk about those limited resources. Yes, it's true that we don't have an exhaustive amount of resources. Given that, we must be strategic in how we manage our resources. While working with a nonprofit dealing with high turnover, I realized a three-month gap in staffing left me with an excess in salaries and benefits. I made the decision to distribute that overage to recruit quality talent, and fairly compensate a team member who had been with the organization for many years but was severely underpaid. I share this example to show that we must be creative in providing financial incentives as a part of our retention strategy. While we don't have unlimited resources, we can be smart about the resources we do have.

As leaders we also must be willing to go to our leadership and board of directors to advocate for better compensation. With a severe mentality of lack, we often **believe** that we just don't have the funds. I emphasize the word believe because what we believe and speak will manifest. We must start speaking excess and abundance; shifting our mindset and taking concrete steps to present a case for competitive compensation as part of our retention strategy. Aligning evidence of the value and impact you and your team are achieving, potential for future growth and your plan for organizational sustainability, will be a strong business case for increased compensation and a robust benefits package. With the right proposal, we can more effectively compensate those who work hard daily to make our organizational mission a reality.

People Are Assets

Beyond the finances, another important factor in retention is being treated as a valued member of the team. Given that we often work in under-resourced situations, it is even more important for those we lead to know what an asset they are. We can't do this work alone. While we might think we are *"Superman"* or *"Superwoman"* – remember we are not. Our teams are equally important to achieving our work and missions.

So, how do you make your team feel valued? There are many ways. One very simple way is to tell them. Let your team know they are appreciated. Those I've worked with know I love to show my appreciation through food and tokens of appreciation. Isn't there an old saying *"the way to a man's heart is through his stomach?"* Well, sometimes the way to a valued team is the treat of a catered lunch, or, even better leaving the office for an extended lunch or afternoon outing. Something that small can have a huge impact. Another way to value your team is in small gifts. And these don't have to be expensive. I recall hearing about one leader who used to leave notes on his team's desks after they had left for the evening. The next morning, they would come into the office greeted by a note of appreciation and gratitude. It truly is that simple.

Another key factor is being vested in your team's development. We must actively seek out and invest in opportunities for our teams to be bond, grow, and develop. Be sure to hold those quarterly retreats where your team can step back and reflect on all that has been achieved. Help them set annual goals for professional and personal development. All of this strongly supports retention.

Culture Matters

A strong retention strategy will either be strengthened or hampered by the cultures we create. We must remain diligent in eliminating toxicity and establishing a healthy culture. Remember, we often spend more time with our colleagues than we spend with our spouses and families. **One study showed that we spend 90,000 hours, over our lifetime, at work (add another 20,000 for school leaders and Executive Directors).** Because we spend so much time with our colleagues, we should enjoy where we work. As strong leaders, it is our job to ensure that enjoyment occurs. We should be the CEO of our organizations – the "Chief Encouragement Officer"

Take another time for reflection: (1) How would you describe your current work culture? (2) Is it inclusive or filled with silos that separate departments and teams? (3) Is it collaborative with shared decision-making? (4) Or is there a single leader making all the decisions and dictating what must happen?

_____
_____
_____
_____
_____
_____
_____

If we are truly committed to retaining high quality talent, we will make the commitment at every level to create an environment that others want to be a part of. A sign of an ideal organizational culture is one with strong leadership, empowered team members, and a commitment to a healthy balance – professionally and personally. As leaders, we should want our respective institutions to be so sound that we have scores of resumes even though we have no available positions. We should be *high quality talent magnets*. Our organizational cultures should attract, train, retain and sustain high quality teams. Doing so is a foundational guarantee to ultimately achieving our goals and impacting the precious commodities we are charged with supporting.

CHAPTER 7

Develop A Support Network
(You Are Not in This Alone)

YOU Matter

I've shared a great deal about what we must do to support those we lead. Now, I want to discuss what we must do to support ourselves. As I've shared, being at the top is not easy, it can be a lonely place. Although leadership is fulfilling, it comes with its own challenges of isolation. Ask yourself: while I'm supporting and advocating for others, who is advocating and supporting me? It's important we are diligent in developing our own support network; creating a delicate and required balance of giving and receiving.

While we work to cultivate healthy and valued teams, sometimes we don't benefit from the same. Often, our level of fulfillment and satisfaction depends on who we report to and their perspectives on leadership. Because of this, learning to "manage up" is important. Even as leaders, we are also accountable to someone. As shared in this article *(What Everyone*

Should Know About Managing Up, www.hbr.org), managing up is not "kissing up". It is knowing how to best navigate your direct manager to ensure that you can achieve what you seek for your team and organization. This is an important skill to master. I am confident that it will make our leadership lives a lot easier.

In addition to managing up, we must also focus on managing out. This is where our support network comes in. While we appreciate and support our teams, we must keep those healthy boundaries. As the leader, we simply cannot share all things with those we lead. It is important to have a network we can confidentially share any challenges we may be facing.

Recommendation #1
Develop a Circle of "Leader Friends"

Connect with Trusted Confidants

A key first step is to develop a circle of colleagues that can be your source of sanity amidst insanity. Connecting with others that can relate to our daily challenges is critically important. Now, don't get me wrong, I am not recommending we come together and complain about everything going wrong at work – although venting is certainly healthy. Rather, I am encouraging us to develop a network of individuals who can help us better navigate our journey of leadership. In developing this circle, an important requirement is trust. We must connect with individuals we respect and trust. Some might be in similar roles as our own. However, our circles should also consist of confidants in different roles – education, government, for profit, non-profit, entrepreneurship. A diversity of perspectives is important.

In my own experience, I have been blessed to connect with groups of women who have traveled a similar path as mine. Many chose to move into the nonprofit world after their careers in business. Others in my circle are what I call "lifers" – friends who have made a commitment to education from the beginning of their careers. What might be considered an outlier in my circle was one of my greatest mentors, a retired partner at my old consulting firm. While he never worked directly in education or nonprofit, he brought a wealth of knowledge on how I could balance everything I was seeking to achieve. This was my circle for many years and many of these folks I still connect with to this very day. Each one brought something different to the table, and I was able to be a blessing to them as well.

Like Attracts Like

Keep in mind that these connections do not always have to be professional; many circles blend into the personal as well. When we can connect with like-minded individuals, we tend to share more of our lives with them. This is an additional benefit to creating this circle – supporting professional development and personal aspirations. This circle truly can serve as a foundation of support that we often go without.

A final consideration in developing this circle is being sure that someone in your circle is "up the ladder" from you. Someone within this group should be a leader who has achieved more than you have. Why, you might ask? Because "like attracts like". If you seek to progress in your professional and personal life, you should surround yourselves with colleagues who has achieved what you seek. These individuals are valuable resources for realizing your long-term goals. We should also look for someone who has successfully balanced all that comes with being an effective leader, and who has conquered the perception that we must sacrifice all else to get there. You might likely serve in that role for others in your circle. That is truly the power of this network. It most certainly is mutually beneficial.

Recommendation #2:
Continually Focus on Your Own Development

As I've shared, as strong leaders we should maintain a continual focus on the development of our teams. But, remember we are a part of that team. We must focus on our own development as well. When we think about development we often think of professional development – specific training that strengthens our leadership skills and subject matter expertise. However, I'm talking about a different form of development: **our own social and emotional development**. In our work, we often talk about the social and emotional development of our students. I again argue that it is the social and emotional development of the adults who support these young people that is even more important.

As I've shared, I firmly believe the challenges we face in education and the nonprofit community are not solely based on the children and communities we serve. Now, hear me out. I know our young people face numerous challenges. I lovingly share - so do we. Many of the difficulties we deal with every day our not child issues, but adult issues. Repeatedly, I've seen how the pain and struggles we deal with as adults detrimentally affects those around us. I recall reading an article about the impact that a depressed teacher can have on their students *(Teacher depression may affect child learning, www.reuters.com)*. In seeing this, it completely made sense to me. Children are like sponges, and they are also very perceptive. They sense our moods; they know when something is wrong; and, they also know if we truly care about them and their success. While reading this article, I had an even greater epiphany. What is the impact of a depressed leader? What must it be like to work within an organization where the leader is dealing with (or not dealing with) his or her own personal struggles? How might this impact those around him/her?

I argue this is even more detrimental because that flows down to every person that leader is responsible for – and ultimately down to those we are called to support. As we've already discussed, our teams are a direct reflection of who we are as leaders. With our own personal challenges and feelings, we can unknowingly project those out to those we lead.

I recall my own challenges in this area. Many years ago, I dealt with bouts of depression. Much of this had to do with my health issues and my attempts to avoid and hide them from those around me. I recall one of my team members candidly sharing with me, that they often waited for me to come in to see what kind of mood I was in. If I was in a good mood, it was going to be a good day. If I was in a bad mood, a not so good day. That was hard for me to swallow, but true. While difficult to accept, this is the kind of negative influence we can have on those we lead.

Eternally grateful for my own healing, this was a very important lesson. That experience taught me that as leaders our own brokenness can have a definitive impact on those we lead and ultimately our careers. That is why I am such a proponent of supporting leaders in becoming whole - spiritually, mentally, physically and emotionally. Some might argue this goes beyond our responsibility. That this crosses personal boundaries. To an extent, that is true. However, I firmly believe we have a responsibility to make sure that in our pathway towards purpose we don't sacrifice our sanity to get there.

Look Within

So, how do we do this? A first step is honest self-reflection. We must take an introspective approach. We must be willing to look within and see those areas that are causing struggles in our own lives. Whether it is something that happened three years ago or thirty years ago - the residue leaves real impact. All of us have had challenges and in some cases very painful experiences in our lives. If we have never dealt with this pain, it will manifest in unexpected ways. One important way is how we interact with and lead others.

In my work, I have observed this impact firsthand. Leaders who have been hurt in their past and are now projecting that hurt out on those they lead. Or, others who have dealt with some form of rejection or abandonment in their childhoods now fear experiencing that same pain as adults. And yet, there are others who are dealing with severe insecurity and compensate by being domineering – attempting to overly control those under their leadership. All of which does nothing but further pain the leader and their teams.

> **Matthew 7:1-3** ~ Judge not, that you be not judged. For with what judgment you judge, you will be judged; and with the measure you use, it will be measured back to you. And why do you look at the speck in your brother's eye, but do not consider the plank in your own eye?

Having walked this path myself, there is no judgement in my spirit - only empathy. I've learned the hard way that while I'm looking at what others are doing wrong, there is a large "plank" sticking out of my own eye I need to address. It is for that very reason that I encourage my clients to focus on their own healing and let God do the same for others. Again, the importance of introspection.

Permission to Heal

In reflecting on inner healing, a friend once shared me with some poignant guidance that I carry into my work. She shared that we must give our parents and elders some grace because they were never given permission to deal with their issues from the past. They were not given the chance to process and heal from tragic circumstances they dealt with years ago. I encourage us to give ourselves and those we lead the same grace. Just because we've struggled to process our pain from the past, does not mean we cannot be healed from those difficulties. As leaders, we might even serve as the catalyst for that healing.

So, with genuine care I encourage us to seek out supports that can help us process personal challenges from our past. Pain that might be unknowingly manifesting in our professional lives. That might include connecting with a trusted therapist or seeking support from your church or place of worship. You can also confide in your "circle of leaders" for support. Whatever the resource, I strongly encourage making this an important priority.

Being leaders does not make us immune to life's challenges. We deal with the same trials as anyone else. It is our role that makes it even more imperative to commit to ensure we achieve the level of health, peace and balance that we deserve. You deserve to take the best care of you – taking your social and emotional care into your own hands will reap a lifetime of benefits.

Recommendation #3
Hire an External Executive/Leadership Coach

Another source of support is an external Executive/Leadership Coach. Clearly, I am a strong advocate for this given my work. Executive coaching is very common in the private sector, where most leaders are assigned leadership coaches early on to support their development. It is less common in our world. I've never really understood why. I'm sure you might be saying it's obvious – back to that lack of resources issue. Yes, financial limitations can sometimes be our reality. However, again I argue we invest in what we consider a priority. If having this type of support is viewed as important, the resources will be there. More importantly, if our managers and board of directors' view this as a priority, they will ensure we have the financial means to receive this support.

Coaching for the Present and Future

One of my most fulfilling coaching experiences was working with a nonprofit leader, who recognized the importance of having someone external help her become a more effective leader and navigate the next steps in her career. We set specific goals and outcomes along with clear evidence of the impact this work would have on the success of her organization. After some negotiation around structure, her manager agreed to make the investment in her leadership development.

Over a six-month period, we made a great deal of progress. One of the first critical steps we took was establishing a relationship of confidence. She felt comfortable confiding in me because my only vested interest was her ultimate success. I did not report to her manager; I reported to her. I was her personal and professional advocate. She could share with me knowing that it would go no further. That was critical to our partnership and the true value of an external coach. While I had a responsibility to report back to my client's manager periodically throughout our engagement, it was only done in a summary format. It was understood that my allegiance was to the leader not to the organization. With that, emphasizing this work was for the betterment of the organization, we went deep both professionally and personally.

My client ultimately ended up receiving a substantial promotion leading her own nonprofit organization. I know, I said it's okay **not** to get promoted. But, in this case that is what my client desired. Thankfully, because of our work together she stepped into her new role with the tools to balance all that came with the position and a substantial pay increase (a very nice side benefit).

Selecting A Coach Is a Personal Choice

Clearly, I think this last recommendation is very important given it is the work of my organization. But, let me be clear, I am not necessarily recommending you hire me or my team. Of course, I would be honored to support you. More importantly, I want you to know you are worthy of making an investment in your own development. You are an asset to your organization and should be treated as such. The resources are there, it just sometimes takes a little creativity and "marketing" to the ones who make those decisions. **If you are that person, I encourage you to vote for YOU.** Make the investment in your own professional and personal development so you can be the best leader possible. There will most certainly be a significant return on your investment, and the greatest return will be your own fulfillment as a **_sustainable leader_**.

CONCLUSION

I truly hope the guidance and recommendations I've provided serve as a valuable resource on your journey of leadership. I applaud your willingness to be that servant leader committed to making a difference in the lives of others. I encourage you to take that same level of commitment to ensure you are living the professional and personal life you deserve. To truly understand that while being of service, it is possible to **_sustain your leadership and your life._**

RECOMMENDED READING

1. Boundaries: When to Say Yes, How to Say No, by Henry Cloud and John Townsend

2. Thrive: The Third Metric to Redefining Success and Creating a Life of Well-Being, Wisdom, and Wonder, by Arianna Huffington

3. The Gifts of Imperfection: Let Go of Who You Think You're Supposed to Be and Embrace Who You Are, by Brené Brown

4. Spirit of Leadership, by Myles Munroe

5. Good to Great: Why Some Companies Make the Leap...And Others Don't, by Jim Collins

6. Soar! Build Your Vision from the Ground Up, by T.D. Jakes

7. The Purpose Driven Life, by Rick Warren

8. Servant Leadership: A Journey into the Nature of Legitimate Power and Greatness, by Robert K. Greenleaf

9. Letting Go: The Pathway of Surrender, by David R. Hawkins MD. PHD

10. Emotional Intelligence: Why It Can Matter More Than IQ, by Daniel Goleman

MEET "BURNED-OUT BRENDA"

"I am truly passionate about education and helping children, but my career choice is taking a real toll on my life. I'm just not sure I can continue to tolerate the stress and overworking that comes with being a nonprofit leader. I am not  *"Superwoman" but I try to be. I know I need to make a change to have more balance and fulfillment in my life but I'm struggling with how. Help!"*

Who You Are: You are in a leadership role in education, government or a nonprofit organization. You made the choice to go into this work to make a difference. You are committed to your work but discouraged and frustrated by all that comes with it. You are becoming more and more disenfranchised, questioning whether sustainable change is possible. Your passion and commitment to making a difference is being overshadowed by the imbalance, politics, agendas and lack of genuine focus on truly making a difference.

What Your Issues Tend to Be: You juggle many balls in the air and fear at some point it's going to all fall apart. You have very little time for yourself and spend most days overwhelmed and exhausted. You know there is more to life than working 12-hour days, evenings and weekends – but are struggling to break that cycle. You want more out of life than just working all the time.

What You Need Most Right Now: You need to connect with someone who has walked in your shoes and intimately knows the challenges you face. You need to be able to confide in someone who is completely outside of your organization or school to share your issues and concerns. I have been in your shoes. Like you, I spent many years working to balance my commitment to education with having a fulfilling life. With so much on my plate I spent most days stressed out, overwhelmed and exhausted. I knew there had to be a better way, I just didn't know how to get to that place. When my health failed from trying to be *"Superwoman"*, I had no choice but to figure it out. I am committed to helping you do the same.

I Can Help: Need support in making these strategies a reality and eliminating burnout in your life? Do not hesitate to reach out to me. I would be more than happy to see how I can support you and your organization once and for all, end **The Burnout Factor™** in your life. I promise you ultimate peace is possible.

Go to http://aprilervin.com/ and schedule a complimentary *"Get Acquainted Call."* I would love to partner with you on this journey and make this a reality in your life.

TESTIMONIALS

"I have worked with many coaches over the years, but few have impacted my life in quite the same way April has. I was at a fork in the road that necessitated a significant life shift. *I COULD NOT have done this without April. I owe her more than I can repay.* – Non-Profit Executive

"April's coaching has been of tremendous benefit to me both personally and professionally. With her guidance, support, and restorative tools, **I was able to discover and remove a HUGE roadblock in my life that was holding up my own progress and complete healing.***"* – Education Entrepreneur

"April has been my "go-to" person as I navigate my journey to find my purpose in life. She listens thoughtfully and then responds in a patient, insightful and inspirational manner." – Government Executive

ABOUT THE AUTHOR

April L. Ervin is **Founder and Chief Peace Officer of Sustainable Leadership, LLC** – a leadership development and executive coaching consulting firm,  dedicated to sustaining effective leadership and healthy organizational cultures. The core mission of the firm is to address the current culture of imbalance, turnover, dysfunction and toxicity and prompt a paradigm shift towards a culture of peace, healing, balance and sustainability.

With more than 15 years of education and nonprofit leadership experience, April intimately knows the opportunities and challenges these leaders face. Like far too many leaders, she spent many years working to the point of exhaustion sacrificing self for the sake of mission. She supports her clients see there is another way. That it is possible to serve your purpose **AND** live a healthy, balanced and fulfilled life.

April has a substantive background in leadership development, nonprofit management, capacity building, strategic planning, project management, fundraising, organizational and operational management. She is an avid believer that a more holistic approach to leadership development will have a transformative impact on the state of education across this country.

April received her undergraduate degree from Northwestern University and MBA from the University of Michigan. She is a highly sought-out speaker and facilitator helping leaders achieve their missions while also creating sustainable organizations.

CONTACT INFORMATION

April L. Ervin, MBA

Chief Peace Officer (CPO)

Sustainable Leadership, LLC

april@aprilervin.com

(872) 223-5675

http://aprilervin.com/

Made in the USA
Lexington, KY
02 November 2018